Healthy plants

Gardening **organically**

One of the great joys of gardening is to experience the variety of life that a healthy garden contains. A garden managed using organic methods will have far more interest in it than a garden where insecticides and chemicals are used. An organic garden is a more balanced environment, where 'good' creatures such as ladybirds and beetles keep the 'bad' pests and diseases under control.

Organically grown plants also tend to be healthier and stronger than plants that rely on large doses of artificial fertiliser. In healthy soil they grow strong roots and can better withstand attack by pests and diseases. Soil can be kept in top condition by recycling garden waste to make nutritious compost. Growing the right combination of plants in the right place at the right time – by rotating where you plant your veg for example, or choosing shrubs to suit the growing conditions that your garden can offer – can deliver impressive disease-free results.

These are the basic principles of organic growing – use the natural resources you already have to create a balanced and vibrant garden. It's sustainable, cheaper than buying chemicals, easier than you think and great fun. Enjoy your organic gardening.

Strong plants resist disease and pests better than plants whose growth is somehow compromised – either by poor soil, lack of light, competition from other plants or lack of water. When you buy plants look for signs of early problems: discoloured foliage, lack of lustre to leaves, stunted growth and pick a healthy specimen. In this book we show you how to keep it healthy using organic methods.

Contents

Why care for plants organically?

Why **care for plants** organically?

Having spent a small fortune on buying plants it's really worth taking good care of them. According to the golden organic rule: prevention is better than cure. But how do you cut down on the wastage that takes place when we plant things in the wrong place, the wrong soil, we fail to prune them or don't give them the conditions they crave? Actually it's easy to look after plants. It's simple and logical. All we really have to do is make certain we meet the plants' need for good soil, water, light and space to grow.

Looking after plants is simple and logical. Make certain that you meet the plants' requirements for soil, water, light and space and you will be off to a good start.

What makes a plant **strong or weak?**

Plants work by taking in water and nutrients through the roots, which fuels growth and photosynthesis. During photosynthesis the plant takes the raw ingredients of water through the roots and carbon dioxide through the leaves, and turns it into sugar and waste oxygen, using the energy of sunlight and a special leaf factory called chlorophyll. Chlorophyll is the green colour in leaves and stems. The manufactured sugar is then stored as starch in every plant cell and used to fuel healthy growth and development.

Plants work by taking in water and nutrients through the roots, which fuels growth and photosynthesis.

Attracting beneficial insects is one way to control pests that attack your plants.

Gardening organically is a proven way of growing plants successfully without the need to use chemicals.

A plant that is provided with the basics of water, nutrients, sunlight and space to grow will generally prosper. A weak plant can result from neglecting these basic needs. A plant lacking these essentials will look unhealthy and be vulnerable to attack by pests and disease or will easily be overcome by weeds.

Gardening organically means growing plants without the aid of man-made fertilisers, through physical removal of weeds instead of using weedkillers and using organic pest and disease controls instead of chemicals. A well cared for garden, where attention is paid to recycling garden waste for compost, will achieve this without too much effort and without needing the addition of artificial fertilisers.

This book shows you some of the easy to use natural methods that will help keep your plants healthy, including maintaining good soil, making your own compost, mulching, pruning, companion planting and making your own liquid fertiliser – a 'comfrey' liquid for example. Get all this right and your friends and family will think you were born with 'green fingers'.

action stations

Why care for plants organically?

1 **Easier gardening** because you harness nature's help

2 **Cheaper** too because you avoid man-made chemicals

3 **Safer** because many of these chemicals can be highly toxic to family, pets, soil and wildlife

4 **More sustainable** because the goodness from kitchen and garden waste is used to nourish your plants

5 **More effective** because organic methods tend to produce healthier plants

Creating conditions
for healthy plants:
soil

New **Beginnings**

Get off to a good start. When you choose plants for the garden look at them carefully. Check for the presence of pests or disease. Gently remove them from the pot and see if the roots are vigorous and well developed but not spiralling out of control and pot-bound. Look for grubs in the compost. If they are present it could indicate a pest problem and the plant should be rejected. The plant should be strong and standing upright. If it is weak and floppy it may be diseased. Look at the colours of the leaves and flowers. Reject any that are discoloured or look tatty. Make sure you're starting off with a healthy, vibrant plant.

Growing from seed can be great fun and rewarding but make sure that the packet is sealed when you buy it. Once the seedlings have germinated don't forget to pot them on when they are big enough and plant out into the garden after the frosts have passed.

Check the plants you buy for health. Avoid tatty, floppy or root-bound examples.

14

Garden **soils**

Know your soil type: The biggest single factor affecting how well your new plants are going to grow, is the soil you place them in. Healthy soil equals healthy plants. Is it a 'heavy' or 'light' soil and what does this mean in terms of growing plants easily? Does your soil have enough water and nutrients? Will it be 'fast' or 'late' to warm up in spring? Basically, soil needs to be well dug over and aerated, free of large lumps and stones and well-drained. This is either easy or difficult to achieve according to what your garden's soil is like now.

Soils can easily be divided into two main types: sandy often called a 'light' soil and clayey called a 'heavy' soil reflecting how easy it is to dig them. To tell which you have in your garden, rub a wet handful between your fingers and thumb having removed all the stones and roots etc. If it feels loose and gritty, it's a sandy soil. If it feels smooth and sticky, it's a clayey soil. In reality, all garden soils are graded somewhere on a continuum between sand and clay so the chances are the soil in your garden will vary. Now all you need to do is learn how to manage it....

Know your soil – it affects what you can grow successfully.

Soil **pH**

pH is a measure of how acid or alkaline the soil is, on a scale from 0 to 14, where **7.0 is neutral**, below 7.0 is acid and above 7.0 is alkaline. Most plants prefer a slightly acid soil of pH 6.5. At this pH, soil organisms including beneficial bacteria, fungus and worms also flourish helping to maintain the garden in perfect balance. Soil pH can range from pH 4.0 to pH 8.0.

Soil pH effects a plant's ability to extract nutrients from the soil and grow healthily. For an example of how pH affects plant behaviour, hydrangeas will produce blue flowers in acid soils of pH 4.0 - 5.0, but pink flowers at pH 6.0 - 7.0.

Rainfall causes the soil to become more acidic. The worst case of acid rain recorded

Soil pH effects a plant's ability to extract nutrients from the soil and grow healthily.

was below pH 3.0. Fizzy drinks are also strong acids around pH 3.0. But some plants prefer acid soils. These are called calcifuge or ericaceous plants and include heathers, rhododendron, camellia, conifers, fuchsia, holly, laurel, magnolia, moss and pyracantha.

Chalky (alkaline) soils are those in which lime (calcium carbonate) is dissolved in the soil water. Hence being called 'limey' soils. If your garden is built on limestone rock or is near a river that floods regularly, you may have alkaline soil. Lime-tolerant plants are called calcicole plants and include astilbe, canna lilies, cotoneaster, crocus, eucalyptus, forsythia, hibiscus, ivy, passion flower, snowdrops and wisteria.

Testing **pH**

To find out the pH of your garden, purchase a test kit from a garden centre. These are very inexpensive and simple to use. You add a small amount of soil from your test area to a test tube and top up with the soil indicator solution included. Then, shake it all up and after the solution has settled, you can compare the resulting colour to a colour chart of known pHs. The one that matches is the pH of your garden. When you take your sample, make sure it is representative of the soil in the garden as a whole.

Liming to reduce acidity

Each year gardens tend to become more acidic. This is caused by acid rain and the acidifying action of micro-organisms, plant roots and leaf fall. That's why every few years you may need to add lime to your garden. Organic gardeners use crushed limestone rock - sold as ground limestone or dolomite limestone - to correct acidity problems. This has the benefit of being slow acting over a period of years. Always check your soil pH before you lime the soil, and follow the instructions on the product packet. Do this slowly but surely, year by year.

Sandy soils

'Hungry' 'early' 'warm' 'light'

Sandy soils are 'light' and the easiest to dig. They come in a variety of colours from very pale yellow to rich rusty red-brown. They are often acid and need regular liming, but have good drainage and plenty of air. However, they may need extra water to avoid drought. The large air spaces warm up quickly in spring and these soils are called 'early' and 'warm' to reflect this. If you're keen on growing vegetables then this early-bird advantage might be just what you need to get mouth-watering home grown veg early in the season.

Sandy soils are also ravenous consumers of organic matter and for this reason they are also called 'hungry', needing extra nourishment to ensure plants grow well. Fortunately, it's easy to do this without breaking the bank. Just dig in plenty of compost and also low nutrient materials such as leafmould.

Plants that hate sandy soils tend to be shallow rooting like summer bedding and flower border plants. Plants that do well in very sandy soils, tend to be able to root more deeply. Examples include some vegetables, including carrots and parsnips, lilies, crab apple, most bulbs, orchids, ornamental grasses, ferns, heathers, cotoneaster, holly, beech and pine. Also look at our section on plants for dry soils.

Sandy soils are ravenous consumers of organic matter. To help improve them, dig in home-produced organic compost made from kitchen and garden waste which breaks down into a nutrient-rich and crumbly earth.

Top tips for sandy soils

1 To follow the organic route, dig in plenty of compost (and leafmould) to to retain water and nourish the soil.

2 Check your pH and add garden lime if necessary.

3 Use wind breaks and mulches to protect the soil against wind erosion.

4 Use fertilisers which are slow release and not so easily washed out of the soil. Mulch the soil well when moist, to help retain water.

5 Grow plants to suit the soil.

6 In dry weather, some plants will require water every few days.

Use a loose covering of organic matter (bark chips or rotted leaves for example) as a mulch to protect the soil from wind erosion, help reduce the spread of weeds and preserve water.

Clayey soils

'Cold' 'late' 'heavy'

Clayey soils provide excellent water reserves and rarely suffer from drought. But although you might save money on your water bill, sometimes they hold on to it too long and extra drainage is needed. Mostly, this is easily achieved by regularly digging over the soil, breaking up any large lumps. These soils are called 'heavy' because they are difficult to dig. The high water content keeps the soil cold in the spring slowing down germination and plant growth, hence being called 'cold' and 'late' soils. They are usually acidic soils and sometimes need the addition of garden lime.

Clayey soils hold large quantities of nutrients and need less fertiliser, making them very useful for growing healthy plants. They are sticky and muddy in the winter then become dry, hard and cracked in hot weather. They shrink when dry and swell when wet. Consequently every effort must be made with these soils to improve their consistency.

Some plants able to tolerate clayey soils include apple, hawthorn, laburnum, forsythia, pyracantha, roses and thuja.

Top tips for **clayey** soils

1 Keep off the garden when the soil is very wet, otherwise you will compact the soil and cause a lack of oxygen and poor drainage to suffocate the roots. Only dig when conditions are right (not too wet or dry).

2 Improve soil the organic way by adding garden compost (preferably home-made). The crumbly texture of compost will help to open up the soil structure thereby encouraging drainage. If drainage is very poor, heap the soil together and grow plants on a raised bed system (this is where you raise the level of soil and build walls around the growing area).

3 Try keeping soil covered with a mulch of bark chips or rotted leaves over winter and at all other times.

4 Keep compost in the top few inches - don't bury it deep – this applies to all soil types.

5 If you dig a hole and it holds water for hours install drainage.

6 Sow seeds later or, in spring, transplant from the greenhouse as seedlings.

Clayey soil benefits from having compost added regularly. In some circumstances it may also need drainage.

action stations

1. **Is your soil sandy or clayey? Take the test.** Rub a wet handful between your fingers and thumb having removed all the stones and roots etc. If it feels loose and gritty, it's a sandy soil. If it feels smooth and sticky it's a clayey soil.

2. **pH testing.** Test your soil to see if it is alkaline or acid. Check that your plants are suitable to grow in that pH and if necessary add garden lime to raise the pH. **Neutral pH is 7, above 7 is alkaline and below 7 is acid.**

3. **Recycle garden and household waste** to build-up a store of compost and mulches. Added to your garden soil they will improve fertiliy, drainage and reduce waterholding the organic way. Apply as a mulch to the surface, or dig in to the top 20cm of soil.

4. **Keep off clayey soil when it's wet.** You will destroy the soil air spaces and compact the soil making it difficult for rain to penetrate and plant roots to grow.

5. **Heavy soils may be dug over in the autumn** and left bare to allow winter frosts to break up the clods. All other soils are best not dug in the autumn, and covered over winter with a mulch or green manure crop.

3

Creating conditions for healthy plants:
water

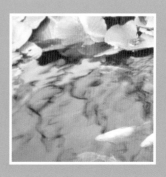

Providing **water**

Plants need lots of water to grow and remain healthy. In fact rather like humans, up to 95% of a plant can be water. It is used not only to maintain cell strength, but also as a raw ingredient for chemical reactions including photosynthesis and to create energy-rich carbohydrates. In seeds, water is used to trigger germination and fuel early growth.

Water is also constantly being lost through the leaves in a process called transpiration. If plants are to remain healthy, additional water must be taken up to replace this loss, otherwise plants will wilt and die.

Providing your garden has been properly managed, including soil preparation, making the correct plant choices and using mulches effectively, there should not be a need for extra watering except in extreme conditions and prolonged hot summers.

Adding water to the garden is best achieved by direct watering of plants in need. However, irrigation can also be useful. Several 'leaky pipe' trickles and 'aqua-tube' products are now available from garden centres to provide a steady drip feed of water. Alternatively, you can simply cut the top off a plastic bottle (the spout and a few inches below) turn it upside down and bury it alongside your plantings. Top this up with water periodically and you have precision watering direct to the roots. Using a watering can with a fine rose, also gives precision delivery with minimal waste.

Don't forget to collect and re-use rain water by fitting water butts to the rainwater downpipes of your house - then wherever it rains fresh water is collected for use on the garden.

Plants for **dry gardens**

If your garden is on dry soil prone to drought, why not take advantage of some beautiful plants that are naturally adapted to survive on less water? Each year our gardens seem to get drier and hotter and water becomes a more precious resource, so managing use of water by plants is very important. Look out for plants with leaves reduced to spines like lavender, the helianthemum or 'rock rose' and rosemary. The reduced leaf surface of these type of plants helps slow down water loss.

Plants like erica and rosemary are able to maintain a moist atmosphere around the leaves by using curled leaves and leaf hairs, again resulting in reduced water loss. Some plants such as kalanchoe and echeveria, have thick juicy leaves perfectly made for water storage. Other favourites include thyme, lavender, hypericum, cotoneaster and sage.

Additional plants that are sun loving and cope with uncertain rainfall include ajuga, berberis, buddleia, foxglove, honeysuckle, sea holly, the rock rose mentioned above, New Zealand flax, poppy and sedums to name but a few. However, don't forget to give your plants extra water when it is really necessary.

Water conservation is becoming more and more important; you can use water butts to collect rainfall or even direct waste bathwater to irrigation! For dry areas consider plants with a reduced leaf area such as lavender.

Top tips to save water in the garden

1 Make shade. Exploit your skills as a garden designer. Strategically place your shrubs and manipulate tree canopies to give protection from the heat and provide a sympathetic backdrop to your plantings.

2 Trim and prune existing plants when necessary. By getting rid of old foliage, the plant is not wasting energy and water feeding old growth.

3 Provide windbreaks in the garden. Try a pergola, decking, netting, wicker screens or architectural plants like New Zealand flax to create this barrier.

4 Mulch-cover bare soil. This will prevent evaporation from the soil, and increase the water reserves available.

5 Install water butts wherever you can. These are often available at a discount from your council or local water company.

Plants for **wet gardens**

If your garden is too wet for healthy plant growth you need to consider a drainage solution. Wet soils starve plant roots of oxygen and encourage disease.

The easiest solution is to heap the soil together and grow on raised banks. Adding in some organic matter will help the process. Sometimes, simply digging over the soil will solve the problem or you might have to be more extreme, such as building a soakaway. You can do this by digging a big hole in the ground and one third fill it with large stones and old bricks, then back fill with soil. Problem solved.

Plants that like wet soils include willow, alder, the stunning rhubarb-like giant gunnera, hostas, flag iris, lobelia, pyracantha, honeysuckle, sedge and astilbes.

Pyracantha will be happy in a wet clayey soil and provides evergreen cover, blossom and berries.

action stations

① **Is your soil dry or wet?** Choose plants that will flourish in your garden.

② **Improve dry soils by...**
- adding bulky recycled compost
- use a mulch covering to add moisture and slow down evaporation from the surface
- erect wind breaks
- select plants that like dry soils.

③ **Improve wet soils by...**
- annually digging over the soil in the autumn
- heap soil into mounds or use raised beds
- dig a soakaway
- dig in organic matter such as rotted leaves or compost
- select plants that like wet conditions.

4 **Select equipment to help with watering**. Choose an efficient method to give your plants just enough water. Also don't forget to collect rainwater in butts for use in the hot weather.

5 **Look at strategies in the garden to reduce the effect of hot weather.** Exploit tall shade plants and erect windbreaks such as wicker panels or wooden structures.

Buddleia is a colourful and interesting wildlife-friendly plant suitable for dry conditions. However, in a smaller garden it may need to be controlled by regular pruning.

The amount of light reaching plants affects their rate of photosynthesis and how vigorously they can grow.

4

Creating conditions for healthy plants:
light

Providing **light**

The amount of light reaching plants affects their rate of photosynthesis and how vigorously they can grow. Plant stems will grow towards light and the roots away from light. A long exposure to light from one side will cause irreversible growth in that direction. Some variegated plants respond to bright light by forming variegation and will lose it if there is not enough light.

In the shade, plants intolerant of shade may grow etiolated (tall, thin and

yellow). This greatly affects the quality of the plant and even if corrective action is taken, an unhealthy appearance remains. Dark shaded patches in the garden are fine for shade loving plants and grasses but don't be disappointed if your prize specimen doesn't grow very well there.

For most plants to remain healthy they need plenty of light. Sadly, our gardens do tend to get over-grown and we need to spend time pruning and thinning plants out. Changing light levels through the seasons also trigger many important plant responses including flowering, leaf fall and dormancy.

As your garden matures, you will find that it gets a little cramped with new plants and old plants that are growing well. Everyone wants an instant garden and we can over-stock the garden in the early years only to have it turn into an out of control wilderness a few years later. In this chapter we look at some of the more common plant growing issues and solutions including pricking-out, potting-on, thinning-out, trimming and pruning.

Reflective surfaces:
An increasingly popular
technique in the garden is to
use reflective surfaces to
maximise available light.

Shade loving garden plants

Azaleas, camellias, clematis, hypericum, mahonia, rhododendron, skimmia, bamboos, Japanese maples, magnolia, hosta, ferns, hellebores, hydrangeas, primrose, lily-of-the-valley, forget-me-nots, bluebell and foxglove.

Bright **sun loving** garden plants

Salvias, achillea, helianthemums (rock rose), campanulas, daisies, hazel, blackthorn, tomatoes, grapes, ceanothus, marigolds, ageratum, amaryllis, apples, arum lily, broom, geraniums and buddleia.

Pricking-out

If you've sown your own seeds or purchased seedling plants, the time will come when they need transplanting into their own containers. This is called pricking-out. When the seedlings are strong enough to handle gently and have produced leaves, they can be transplanted into fresh compost and bigger pots. Take great care to lift them carefully by the stem.

Many ferns thrive in damp, shady corners and provide striking architectural interest.

Potting-on

Plants grown in containers have limited root space and need periodic potting-on into bigger pots or outdoors into the soil. If they are not potted-on, the roots will spiral round the container slowly suffocating the plant and they are said to be 'pot-bound'. At this point, even if they are freed and planted into the soil, their life span will be significantly shorter. Pot-bound conifers for example, often only live for 10 years when eventually planted out into soil.

Take care when potting-on to position the plant in the middle of the container and use only fresh compost. When the weather is warm and they are big enough, they can be planted out into your garden.

Plants grown in containers have limited root space and need periodic potting-on into bigger pots or outdoors into the soil.

Consider using bark chips as both a mulch, weed barrier and a technique to complement the visual appearance of your garden.

Thinning-out

If your garden is getting overgrown you simply have to get stuck in and hack away till you have removed the overstocked plants. As this involves evicting unwanted plants this can be done at any time of year, but take care not to damage the foliage or roots of plants you want to keep. Also, cut out and dispose of any diseased or pest ridden plants by burning or putting into the kerbside collection bin if you have one. Recycle all other waste material into the compost heap so that you have a supply of organic matter to use as a mulch next year.

Organic matter is any semi-rotted natural plant material that can be spread on the garden where it will provide useful cover, preventing weeds and helping retain moisture. If this material is allowed to rot for longer in the compost heap it will become compost.

Trimming and Pruning

All woody plants need trimming and pruning at one time or another. The best time to do this is in the winter between November and February. Not only does this enable you to shape the plant as you wish, but also removes the old leaves which may be discoloured and unsightly. Trimming and pruning also stimulates fresh new growth that looks bright and shiny. There is no mystery about how to prune. Just cut the stem above a leaf joint, leaving a downwards slope so that rainwater can run off. That's it, it's that simple.

With roses prune off the flower after it has been open for a few days. It takes plants an incredible amount of energy to keep a flower going and in pruning it you remove this demand and encourage the rose to put its spare energy into new bud formation. You can keep doing this throughout the season for an everlasting supply of fresh flowers for your house.

Dead-head roses regularly to keep new blooms coming.

Pruning fruit trees does require care and different fruits need different approaches. We would recommend seeking specific guidance on each type of fruit. However, as a general rule, fruit trees should be pruned just once a year when the plant is dormant between November and February.

Laurel and conifer hedges are probably the most abused plants of all, being allowed to grow uncontrollably into the monstrous trees that they can be. With just a little care they can look stunning and are easily managed. The correct technique is to trim back the side growth and prune back the main stem by at least 30 cm. This can be done in the spring and summer. This action alone will stimulate the laurel to produce new side shoots and leaf buds creating an ever more dense wall of shiny green leaves. Take care though with leyland cypress – you should not cut these back to old wood as they do not always re-grow.

Laurel makes a vigorous and dense visual screen.

Trim and prune plants just above leaf joints to encourage fresh vigorous re-growth, shaped as required. Don't let hedges grow uncontrollably.

Top tips to alter garden light levels

At first sight this may seem an impossible task. However, for centuries gardeners have been practising the craft of maximising light through techniques of good plantsmanship.

1 **Plant spacing**. By regulating how close plants are to each other you can either increase or decrease the light falling on the lower leaves. The more light, the more photosynthesis and the healthier the plant. Make sure your plantings are not bunched up together and overcrowded. Not only will this hinder growth but it also provides a motorway network of leaves over which pests and disease can spread.

2 **Remove weeds**. Weeds compete for light, water and nutrients. Inspect your garden regularly and remove anything that you haven't planted or don't want growing. You can pull them up by hand, use a hoe or small trowel to do this.

3 **Shading**. Some plants are happy with low light levels and you can stimulate their growth by providing shading to that piece of the garden. Use tall architectural trees and shrubs or man-made structures like wicker panels to increase shade.

4 **Reflective surfaces**. An increasingly popular technique in the garden is to use reflective surfaces. This can be as simple as painting walls or fence panels with bright coloured paints to reflect the light over the plantings. For strawberries, try planting through a white polythene sheet. It will reflect the light back up onto the leaves. Increasingly, other methods such as using mirrors or other reflective metals near ponds are growing in popularity but do consider the problems these may cause for birds and wildlife before using them.

5 **Orientation of greenhouse or garden**. If you are able to exploit your garden so that key growing areas are south facing, it will get the sun all day. For the same reason greenhouses should be positioned on an east-west axis.

Man-made structures such as fence panels can help to increase shade.

action stations

1 **Walk your garden** and identify areas that are getting too wild. Plan which areas need thinning out and what plants should go where. Thin-out dense garden growth from overcrowded beds.

2 **Trim and prune** plants just above leaf joints to encourage fresh vigorous re-growth. Don't let hedges grow uncontrollably.

3 **Weeding.** Inspect the garden regularly and remove any plants you don't want. These plants will be competing for light, water and nutrients.

4 **Thin out** plants that are too crowded so that light can penetrate to the lowest leaves and perhaps use reflective materials around the shaded patches.

5 **Houseplants** in the home and greenhouse will greatly benefit from clean window panes. Make sure these plants are in rooms with high or low light levels according to their requirements.

5

Maintaining healthy plants and garden

Keeping your soil and plants healthy does not require the addition of artificial fertilisers or chemicals. Just follow the basic principles of organic gardening – create compost from waste materials, rotate your crops to reduce soil borne diseases and pests, give plants the conditions they like and look after your soil. The rest will happen naturally.

Maintaining **healthy soil**

Compost

Soil can be improved by adding compost, leafmould, well rotted manure and other forms of organic matter. These additions will encourage soil bacteria and fungus that are critical in the ecosystem of the soil, especially in maintaining pH and gluing the soil together into a desirable crumb structure.

To make organic compost, start piling all your garden and kitchen waste onto a compost heap or into a compost making bin.

The types of waste to put on the compost heap include grass clippings, prunings, weeds, bark, leaves, paper, egg shells, peelings and vegetable waste from the kitchen. To be successful the heap needs a good supply of carbon from woody material, bacteria and fungi. Generally the more finely chopped your waste, the faster it will compost. Don't use pest or disease-infected plants, too many perennial weeds, fish or meat waste.

For more about creating compost see *Create Compost* in the *Green Essentials* series.

Mulching

A mulch is a dressing of bulky organic material, spread on the soil surface in the spring and summer to suppress weeds, conserve water, add nutrients and encourage earthworm activity. Mulch is also useful in winter for soil protection.

Straw is often used as a mulch when growing strawberries to prevent the fungal disease called grey mould from splashing onto the fruit from the soil.

The best approach is to use compost material as a mulch – it removes the need to use weedkillers, pesticides or inorganic fertilisers. Other mulches to use include leafmould, grass clippings, bark and even appropriate synthetic mulches or barriers to control weeds.

For more guidance on organic composting see *Create Compost* in the *Green Essentials* series.

Digging

Too much digging is not only tiring but it may not be necessary. Whilst digging can improve both drainage and aeration and is a good way of adding organic matter, it can also disturb soil fauna and turn up weed seeds. After digging the soil should be raked level, this will leave the surface neat and level with a crumb-like covering of fine soil.

When digging, also chop up and bury annual weeds like chickweed, groundsel and speedwells, but perennials like creeping thistle, couch grass and yarrow, should be removed and disposed of.

• don't dig light soils unless vital

• digging clay is hard work – try improving with organic matter instead

Light soils may not need digging. Heavy soils can be improved with the addition of organic matter.

Nutrition

To grow well, plants need a supply of nutrients including nitrogen (N) for growth; phosphorus (P) for strong root growth and potassium (K) for cell strength and resistance to disease. All three nutrients are also involved in flowering and fruiting. Normally these nutrients are adequately supplied by using your own compost and mulches. Other nutrients include magnesium, calcium and sulphur. Trace elements may include iron, manganese, copper, zinc, boron and molybdenum. The regular addition of organic matter (decaying living plant and animal remains) and manure should keep these soil nutrients in balance.

Some signs of nutrient deficiency:

Nitrogen: Pale green to yellow leaf colour and stunted growth.

Phosphorus: Purple leaf edges and poor root growth.

Potassium: Yellow leaf colour starting at the edges and spreading in to the middle covering the whole leaf. Stems are weak and floppy.

Where possible, buy a certified product with a recognised organic logo such as that of the HDRA or the Soil Association.

More about organic fertilisers

Use fertilisers made from natural materials. They are slowly broken down in the soil to feed your plants steadily. These fertilisers are useful on poor soils, and when you don't have enough compost or manure to feed all the plants that need it. Artificial fertilisers on the other hand create a 'quick fix' but then lead to the need to use more and more chemicals as the life in the soil actually diminishes.

- Chicken manure pellets

- Potash of plant origin

- Blood, fish and bone meal (mainly for propagating)

- Blended general fertilisers

- Hoof and horn meal

- Seaweed meal (from sustainable sources)

- Rock phosphate

Plant and mineral based fertilisers are available for those who prefer to avoid animal based products.

Always use as directed on the packet.

Plant **tonics** and liquid feeds

There are several products available that can help build up natural resistance in plants. These include:

Seaweed extract which contains a number of trace elements and natural plant growth stimulants – these combine to promote healthy plants which then become more proficient in their uptake of nutrients and consequently less susceptible to pest and diseases.

Seaweed and iron for specific iron deficiencies encountered on chalky soils.

Liquid comfrey – a good all purpose vegetable feed that works well with peppers and tomatoes. Why not grow comfrey and make your own feed?

In addition, there are a number of general certified organic liquid feeds and fertilisers aimed at specific crops such as tomatoes or formulated for general use on plants, flowers and vegetables. Check that any product you purchase is certified as organic – ask your supplier if you are in any doubt.

Pest **control**

Organic gardening is based on the principle that a healthy plant is much less likely to become the target of a pest or disease attack. So if you have followed the advice in this book you will already be well ahead of the enemy.

Pests either damage plants by biting and chewing, such as slugs and the vine weevil; or they damage by sucking the sap, such as whitefly and aphids. Sap-sucking insects tend to cause white marks on leaves and flowers and encourage disease as they excrete a concentrated sugar solution from their bodies and on which fungal infections feed.

Some pests can be discouraged by creating physical barriers. For more information, see the *Green Essentials* book *Control Pests* for more detailed information on this important topic.

Ground beetles, wasps, lacewings and the larvae and adult of the ladybird will help to provide an effective arsenal against garden pests.

Encouraging the **natural enemies** of pests

It is a fundamental principle of organic gardening to exploit nature's own power to safely control common pests. This is simpler to accomplish than might at first appear to be the case. In essence all organisms have a need for food and shelter. If these can be provided and tailored to the preferences of specific natural enemies, then their populations will rise as they move into the neighbourhood.

Top of the list of desirable natural enemies (often called biological controls if you buy them in from specialist suppliers) to have as lodgers are a cohort of powerful predators including hoverflies, ladybirds, ground beetles and lacewings, together with parasitic wasps. Combined, these will provide an effective arsenal against caterpillars, aphids, slugs and other pests.

Also try and keep some areas of the garden for dense tussock-forming grasses like cocksfoot and yorkshire fog – you can either sow these or leave an area unmown. These conditions are adored by beetles and spiders, who will swarm over your garden in spring, launching devastating attacks on all available pests.

Birds are remarkably civilised. Install a bird feeder and they will queue to feed, but while they wait they will feed on the pests that may be damaging your plants.

Flying insects like ladybirds and hoverflies are encouraged by providing areas of rough vegetation, hollow stems, twigs and by leaving part of the garden unkempt. However these beneficial insects also like herbaceous borders and cultivated flowers. In large numbers hoverflies can give total control against aphids. Also planting wild flowers by fences or hedgerows will greatly increase the number of beneficial insects visiting and feeding in your garden. These unkempt areas can also provide overwintering accommodation for lacewings and ladybirds providing you with an on-site army of biological agents ready for the next season.

For more on organic pest control methods see *Control Pests* in the *Green Essentials* series.

Visiting birds will happily feed on garden pests.

Beneficial insects such as ladybirds and hoverflies will be encouraged by providing a wildlife area in your garden.

Some flowers to grow to **attract pest eating insects**

Hoverflies, wasps, ladybirds and flower bugs are some of the insect predators that will help control pests - attract them by planting some of the following near your vegetable patch or vulnerable plants:

- Cornflower
- Gazania
- Corn marigold
- Sunflower
- Fennel
- Nemophila
- Californian poppy
- Poached egg plant
- Pot marigold
- Annual convolvulus
- French marigolds
- Yarrow

Companion planting

Companion planting is another organic technique for keeping pests and diseases at bay. The theory is that certain combinations of plants can help growth and reduce pest or disease problems. Companion planting works in different ways, for example:

- repelling insects by giving off natural chemicals or scent
- attracting beneficial insect predators and pollinators
- as decoys to keep pests away from a vulnerable main crop
- absorbing minerals and/or fixing nitrogen in the soil
- creating shade or a windbreak and providing ground cover.

Companion planting is worth trying, with the proviso that there is no hard and fast evidence that all the 'companionships' suggested in books are effective. Try out some of the suggestions below making sure the companions don't compete for food and water., but do be prepared to use other organic methods if needs be.

French marigolds to repel whitefly from greenhouse tomato crops.
Onions to repel carrot fly.
Sweetcorn to provide shade for summer lettuce.
Interplanting cabbages with an unrelated plant such as french beans to repel aphids and whitefly.
Dill to attract hoverflies and wasps which eat aphids.
Garlic as deterrent for aphids, this is particularly good to plant with roses.

Help from a **pond**

Putting in a pond will bring some of the best help to bear on any pests you have. Frogs and toads eat slugs, dragonflies eat flying insects. Choose a sunny open spot, not overhung by trees or bushes, but with a hedge or fence nearby to offer some shelter. Using a flexible plastic or butyl (rubber) liner is the easiest means of construction, or if space is very tight a pre-formed plastic pond. For more information on how to build a pond see the *Green Essentials* title, *Create Ponds*.

Natural resources

As has been seen throughout this book, keeping plants healthy depends not on unattainable levels of skill, but on applying some simple organic gardening techniques to improve conditions for your plants.

Plant care is not difficult, but it does require the gardener to take a close look at his or her garden. Try and plan ahead and do the simple things right.

Use the natural resources available to you and your garden should flourish.

action stations

1 **Inspect plants for signs of nutrient deficiency.** Look for stunted growth, pale yellow or purple leaves, floppy stems and poor root growth.

2 **Use only slow-releasing fertilisers** such as hoof and horn, bone meal and ground rock potash, seaweed extract etc.

3 **Grow your own liquid fertiliser.** Collect the leaves of your **comfrey plant** and squeeze the highly concentrated sap out. Dilute 1:15 with water for a perfect plant fertiliser.

4 **Encourage pest enemies** into the garden through providing mounds of soil, tussock-forming grasses and rough vegetation as a home for nature's army of beneficial insects.

5 **Companion planting.** Mix and match plants to attract beneficial insects and make best use of light, space and water.

6 **Build your compost heap.** Either start a heap or purchase a compost bin. Recycle garden and household waste into the bin adding a layer of soil once in a while.

who, what, where, when and why organic?

for all the answers and tempting offers go to www.whyorganic.org

- Mouthwatering offers on organic produce
- Organic places to shop and stay across the UK
- Seasonal recipes from celebrity chefs
- Expert advice on your food and health
- Soil Association food club – join for just £1 a month

Soil Association
the heart of organic food & farming

Resources

HDRA the organic organisation promoting organic gardening farming and food
www.hdra.org.uk
024 7630 3517

Soil Association the heart of organic food and farming
www.soilassociation.org
0117 929 0661

MAIL ORDER:

The Organic Gardening Catalogue
Organic seeds, composts, raised beds, barriers, traps and other organic gardening sundries.
All purchases help to fund the HDRA's charity work.
www.organiccatalogue.com
0845 1301304

Agralan Ltd
www.agralan.co.uk
01285 860015

Centre for Alternative Technology
www.cat.org.uk
01654 705950

Rooster – Greenvale Farms Ltd
Organic fertiliser
www.rooster.uk.com
01677 422953

Tamar Organics
www.tamarorganics.co.uk
01822 834887

The Wormcast Company
Organic fertiliser
www.thewormcastcompany.com
0845 605 5000

Want more organic gardening help?

Then join HDRA, the national charity
for organic gardening, farming and food.

As a member of HDRA you'll gain-
- free access to our Gardening Advisory Service
- access to our three gardens in Warwickshire, Kent
  and Essex and to 10 more gardens around the UK
- opportunities to attend courses and talks or visit
  other gardens on Organic Gardens Open Weekends
- discounts when ordering from the Organic
  Gardening Catalogue
- discounted membership of the Heritage
  Seed Library
- quarterly magazines full of useful information

You'll also be supporting-
- the conservation of heritage seeds
- an overseas organic advisory service to help
  small-scale farmers in the tropics
- Duchy Originals HDRA Organic Gardens for Schools
- HDRA Organic Food For All campaign
- research into organic agriculture

To join HDRA ring: **024 7630 3517**
email: **enquiries@hdra.org.uk**
or visit our website: **www.hdra.org.uk**

Charity No. 298104